Christmas

What day is it?

HAPPY HOLIDAYS!

Christmas

by Pearl Markovics

Consultant:
Beth Gambro
Reading Specialist
Yorkville, Illinois

Contents

BEARPORT
PUBLISHING

New York, New York

It is Christmas!

It is Christmas.

I see the tree.

It is Christmas.

I see the lights.

It is Christmas.

I see the gifts.

It is Christmas.

I see the cookies.

It is Christmas.

I see the stockings.

It is Christmas.

What do you see?

Key Words

cookies

gifts

lights

stockings

tree

Index

About the Author

Pearl Markovics loves holidays of every kind—especially the ones that include sweets and lots of presents.

Teaching Tips

Before Reading

- ✔ Guide readers on a "picture walk" through the text by asking them to name the things shown.

- ✔ Discuss book structure by showing children where text will appear consistently on pages.

- ✔ Highlight the supportive pattern of the book. Note the consistent number of sentences and words found on each page.

During Reading

- ✔ Encourage children to "read with your finger" and point to each word as it is read. Stop periodically to ask readers to point to a specific word in the text.

- ✔ Reading strategies: When encountering unknown words, prompt readers with encouraging cues, such as:

  - **Does that word look like a word you already know?**
  - **It could be _____ , but look at _____ .**
  - **Check the picture.**

After Reading

- ✔ Write the key words on index cards.

  - **Have readers match them to pictures in the book.**
  - **Have children sort words by category (words that end with *s*, for example).**

- ✔ Encourage readers to talk about other holidays.

- ✔ Ask readers to identify their favorite page in the book. Have them read that page aloud.

- ✔ Ask children to write their own sentences about a holiday. Encourage them to use the same pattern found in the book as a model for their writing.

Credits: Cover, © 2M media/Shutterstock; 1, © Mark Umbrella/Shutterstock; 2–3, © 1tomm/Shutterstock; 4–5, © PinkyWinky/Shutterstock and © Smileus/Shutterstock; 6–7, © Fotomicar/Shutterstock; 8–9, © infografick/Shutterstock; 10–11, © Africa Studio/Shutterstock and © Irina Mitin/Shutterstock; 12–13, © Valentina Proskurina/Shutterstock; 14–15, © Romiana Lee/Shutterstock; 16T (L to R), © Africa Studio/Shutterstock, © Irina Mitin/Shutterstock, and © infografick/Shutterstock; 16B (L to R), © Fotomicar/Shutterstock, © Valentina Proskurina/Shutterstock, and © Smileus/Shutterstock.

Publisher: Kenn Goin **Senior Editor**: Joyce Tavolacci **Creative Director**: Spencer Brinker

Library of Congress Cataloging-in-Publication Data in process at time of publication (2019)
Library of Congress Control Number: 2018023625
ISBN-13: 978-1-64280-113-2 (library binding) | ISBN-13: 978-1-64280-148-4 (paperback)

10 9 8 7 6 5 4 3 2 1